REDSEA
THE SAUDI COAST

CHRISTOPHER SMITH

REDSEA
THE SAUDI COAST

ASSOULINE

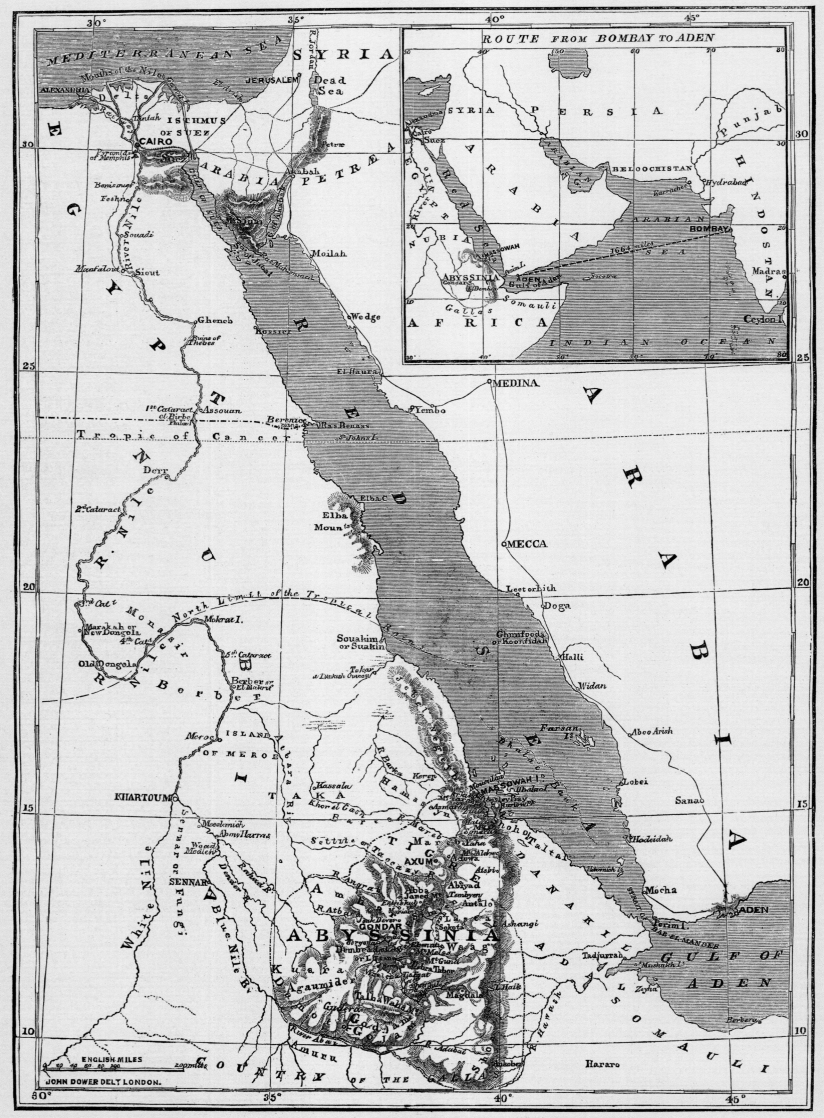

ABYSSINIA AND THE SHORES OF THE RED SEA.

INTRODUCTION

The Red Sea is an eternal mystery that knows how to keep its secrets. Its mystery lies in its spellbinding power, its power to seduce, but always softly, subtly and discreetly. And, I would maintain, it makes the Red Sea all too often the subject of misconceptions.

The Red Sea is separate from the Mediterranean. But everything conspires to make us think of it as its matrix, or at least its offshoot, if not its glittering reflection, with its sleepy towns, holy sites and fabled cities. For the Red Sea is anything but a dead sea. It positively teems with life. The major routes of the Arabian Peninsula have beaten a path to it for millennia, while along its shores the Romans scattered ports that are no longer celebrated, as though history had covered its tracks precisely to preserve the great mystery of the sea. Writers—and distinguished ones at that—have lost themselves here in order to find themselves again, far from any coteries. The three religions of the Book find mutual connections, and civilizations have reinvented their myths here. In short, the Red Sea carries symbolic power.

A MELTING POT OF CIVILIZATIONS, FAITHS AND HOPES

The Red Sea is thus—once we get beyond any misconceptions—a melting pot of civilizations, faiths and hopes. It is another Mediterranean, or "Mare Nostrum," as the Romans called it. The Romans' name for the Red Sea was "Mare Rubrum." It, too, separates and unites two continents, and it, too, has seen monotheistic faiths grow up on its shores. I recall its scarlet reflections of the surrounding mountains and its blooms of the red algae *Trichodesmium erythraeum*, having many times crossed this long watery expanse of submerged treasures—described with such peerless narrative skill in Arabic folktales—from its African shores to its eastern coasts, from the Horn of Africa to Arabia Felix. From the very first encounter, I was entranced by its crystalline clarity, its dizzying transparency (reaching down two hundred meters in places) and its pristine coral reefs, whether viewed from land or sea. Its limpid waters always induce the same bewitching feeling, an enchantment that is impossible to define. Is it the shimmering reflections of the setting sun, in endless ripples, that inflame our imagination? Or is it the pristine beauty of its little-visited shores? Or the magic of the novels by major writers who have spent time on its shores, from Arthur Rimbaud to Joseph Conrad, and from Joseph Kessel to Romain Gary?

The purity of the light and the untouched beauties of nature are magnified on its shores. This sea that laps the coastlines of eight countries is a chameleon sea, not just red but also green, gray, blue and black, following the whims of the light and the moods of the sun. Towns that shimmer in shades of silver, ancestral ports where pirates moored their sambuks, wild inlets where nature still reigns unchallenged, extinct volcanoes with their scatterings of black stones, villages of ancient dwellings, relics of the caravansaries of the incense roads and coral reefs teeming with fish remind us that the living world is not just the preserve of humans. Ruined ramparts mingle with solitary minarets. Tales of the Orient seem to lie spread out before you, deploying all their charms and bewitching spells. Sails cut a path across the seascape, topping wooden vessels—dhows and feluccas—that look fragile but are sturdy and seaworthy, carrying the descendants of the great mariners, pearl dealers, nakhodas, navigators and pirates who once scoured these waters down to the Cap des Aromates, now merchants, sailors, fishermen and simply travelers to tropical waters.

These are the worthy heirs of the Greek explorer Hippalus, who in the first century CE sailed the route between the Erythraean Sea (the Greek term for "Red Sea") and India, using the monsoon winds. When the hot northwesterly winds (shamals) blew, the waves seemed to become filled with grains of sand, like a gift from a mischievous djinn. This is the fate of waters that separate invasive deserts, from the eastern Sahara to the Ar-Rub Al-Khali. Sometimes the distant dunes and mountains take on a savage air, catching fire and turning an incandescent red, from Sinai to Eritrea and from Egypt to Arabia, highlighted by an archipelago where quantities of pearls were once hunted and now birds find shelter—flamingos, raptors and pelicans. Every year, over a million and a half migrating birds of nearly forty species fly between Africa's Rift Valley and the Red Sea. This patchwork of many colors cannot help but stir the imagination, even in the midst of the sea, when the two shores seem to come closer to each other and the two continents to embrace.

A STRANGE ALCHEMY
BETWEEN DREAM AND REALITY

People have managed to protect these shores, at once so widely explored and yet so largely overlooked. At the crossroads of continents, Saudi Arabia has been an extraordinary meeting point for civilizations that left behind an important heritage. The Kingdom also offers an impressive biodiversity, with some of the most unusual animals on Earth, with birds like the hammerkop, crab plover and hypocolius. Major initiatives have been undertaken by Saudi Arabia to preserve the Red Sea and its unique biodiversity, including initiatives to conserve marine life, as well as programs at the Faculty of Marine Sciences at King Abdulaziz University and the Saudi Aquaculture Society. With a new approach to sustainable development, the Red Sea Development Company, a Saudi national program, is pursuing a set of ambitious but tangible environmental goals, such as achieving a 30 percent net conservation "plus" in the Red Sea by 2040 and, remarkably, obtaining 100 percent of Saudi Arabia's energy from renewable sources, most notably large-scale microalgae farms. Implemented over 28,000 square kilometers of pristine lands and waters along Saudi Arabia's west coast, and particularly on ninety islands, this huge project combines environmental, economic and societal components, and aims to create one of the world's most ambitious and innovative tourist destinations.

These projects envision an exciting future for the Red Sea coast, but tales from the past also fire our imaginations. Here more than elsewhere, the historical accounts of explorers and adventurers are more than a match for the fictional depictions, sometimes penned by the same authors. It's as if the Red Sea allows this curious alchemy, this symbiosis between the tangible and the dream-like that is fundamentally the distinguishing feature of every civilization. From this matrix there thus emerges a space that is unique, that can leave no traveler unmoved. For is adventure not the very essence of fiction? And the Red Sea is an adventure in itself, as much now as it was then.

A beautiful small port in Saudi Arabia, Al Wajh is a perfect example of the links between the two sides of the sea. As in other fabulous localities in the northwestern part of the Kingdom, Al Wajh shows the harmony of craftsmen's talents. Today, we can find quiet beaches around the city, with seafood restaurants and exciting diving trips, too.

In fact, the fabled lands along the shores of the Red Sea have always enticed travelers—not just conquerors and navigators but writers and adventurers on a quest for a new Holy Grail. First, there was the poet Rimbaud, who produced virtually his entire literary output between the ages of seventeen and nineteen, revolutionizing poetry and literature and summoning the world into his verses before abruptly withdrawing from it: "*Je est un autre*" ("I is an other"). Where should he choose to spend the remaining twenty years of his life? After escapades in Cyprus and Java, he put his finger on a globe; it pointed to the Red Sea. With the ambition of living out his *Illuminations*, the title of his incomplete suite of mostly prose poems, he spent the rest of his days, until his death in 1891, at the age of thirty-seven, sailing back and forth across the Red Sea, landing in Jeddah, Djibouti, Harar (in Abyssinia) and Aden—as though all his poetry would find one or several home ports on this vast stretch of water, fertile ground for myths and, above all, for Bible stories. The "I is an other" of the visionary poet became "I am from elsewhere." The Rimbaud of Abyssinia was first and foremost the Rimbaud of the Red Sea. I have always been so struck by this, in discussions with his biographers and in my own travels following in his footsteps.

Such genius! No wonder the Rimbaud of the Red Sea still inspires so many writer-travelers. A writer's horizons comprise an atlas of ports of call conjured in dreams. Arriving is not what matters; all that counts is slipping out of our moorings. During his prolonged adventure, Rimbaud could only write his legend, which was inseparable from his poems. When he entered the Suez Canal on his way to discover the Red Sea, he was embarking on a new life. As he wrote in his poem "The Impossible," "It is of Eden that I was dreaming!" This sea was to complement his poetry, or rather to magnify it. *A Season in Hell*, his major work, became a season of heading for paradise, even if it was strewn with pitfalls.

Of course, the towns and ports have changed since Rimbaud sailed these waters, but their spirit lingers on. My own travels took me to the Red Sea of the *poète voyant*, the poet prophet, in Port Sudan, Al Hudaydah, Sawakin and elsewhere, as far as the Eritrean highlands. "I have looked for work in the Red Sea ports, at Jeddah, Sawakin, Massawa, Hudaydah, etc.," Rimbaud wrote home on August 17, 1880, in thirty-five-degree (Celsius) heat from Aden, where he was drinking distilled seawater after "rolling about on the Red Sea." The adventurer was breathing new life into the destiny of the *poète maudit*.

THE RED SEA ROUTES, THE OTHER SILK ROADS

This link between Rimbaud's poetry and his adventures demonstrates the formidable nature of the matrix that is the Red Sea, the bridge of millennia between civilizations, religions and cultures. The footpaths and caravan trails of Arabia Felix were also pathways to knowledge and understanding. For centuries, overnight stops at caravansaries along the Silk Road gave travelers from distant places opportunities to exchange not only goods such as gold, silk and lapis lazuli but also ideas. Similarly, the Red Sea routes opened pathways to symbiosis, vectors for the living memory of humanity.

It was a celebration that I found in a few Red Sea ports, and even at the foot of Mount Sinai, in the Monastery of St. Catherine. All around it, the slopes hurtle down from an altitude of one to two thousand meters to sea level, as though answering the call of the distant waves or an invitation to explore the depths, as if this warm sea were in love with the cool mountains, which are as high as its abysses are deep. On the Saudi Arabian coast, you feel you might glimpse the shadows of the dromedary trains of T. E. Lawrence, dubbed "Lawrence of Arabia" and described by Winston Churchill as "one of those beings whose pace of life was faster and more intense than the ordinary."

THE FABULOUS JOURNEY OF THE QUEEN OF SHEBA

The legendary journey of the Queen of Sheba to visit King Solomon, son of David, as described in the Bible and the Koran, has also contributed to the mirage-like history of this region. Known as "Balqis" in the Islamic world and as "Makeda" in Ethiopia, the Queen of Sheba is first mentioned in the First Book of Kings in the Old Testament and in Saba, the thirty-fourth surah of the Koran, as well as in An-Naml (the Ant), the twenty-seventh surah. The similarities between the religions of the Book regarding this encounter are

astonishing. In the twenty-seventh surah of the Koran, Balqis is not named. Her story, at the heart of a widespread cycle of legends, has been embellished by commentators, their origins placed in southern Arabia. According to the twenty-seventh surah, Solomon, informed by one of his birds that Al-Malika Balqis ("with a magnificent throne") is worshipping the sun, asked her to worship Allah and invited her to visit. Then, fascinated by the king and the magnificence of Al-Quds, or Jerusalem, she converted to the Solomon religion.

Coming from a legendary land on the shores of the Red Sea, surrounded by mountains, desert and the open sea, and rich in aromatic plants, spices, salt, henna, lavish jewels, feminine accoutrements, richly sewn garments and wood carvings, the "queen of the south" was lavish in her gifts and accompanied by "a very large entourage, camels laden with aromatics, gold in enormous quantities, and precious stones" (1 Kings 10:2). As Gustave Flaubert, who nursed a passion for the Orient, wrote in *The Temptation of Saint Anthony*, "The Queen of Sheba, knowing the fame of Solomon, came to tempt him with riddles." For his part, the great king of unfathomable wisdom made no secret of his riches, but his interest in the kingdom of Sheba, south of the Red Sea, was further piqued by the recent return of one of his embassies with over four hundred gold talents from the land of Ophir, just to the north.

Nobody knows the exact whereabouts of the port of Ophir—possibly present-day Eilat or Aqaba, at the gates of the Arabian desert or perhaps on the African coast of the Red Sea—but it was the northern pendant of the land of Sheba, and exerted the same fascination over the powerful rulers of the Orient. The figure of Balqis as a sovereign woman is that of a just and enlightened monarch, according to the Koran. The portrait is therefore that of a leader fond of equity and justice. The Koranic verses are explicit about this illustrious woman's way of governing.

After this the Ptolemies, skilled navigators and conquerors, succeeded in diverting the Silk Road and loading their boats with precious stones, metals, spices and silk to transport across the Red Sea back to Egypt.

According to the reports of Portuguese explorers in the late fifteenth century, Abyssinia was also the kingdom of the legendary Prester John, a Christian sovereign of fabulous wealth who was willing to offer help to western travelers and protection to major maritime expeditions. Rumors of the existence of the kingdom of Prester John, which had reached the Old World with the Crusaders, became entrenched as certain truth and gave rise to covetous dreams of untold riches, especially after the ruler of Ethiopia sent an embassy to the papal court in the early fourteenth century. Explorers and adventurers were ready to risk all to reach this hypothetical paradise, at a time when the El Dorados of the Americas had not yet been "discovered" by the Europeans. It was the end of the Middle Ages and the beginning of the Renaissance. And the Red Sea was the New World.

FROM IBN BATTUTA TO RIMBAUD

These were the tales that drove so many of my journeys through the region. At Al Hudaydah, after crossing the coastal plain of Tihama, the "low land" that is one of the hottest places on the planet, where Pier Paolo Pasolini chose to film his *Arabian Nights*, I felt the atmosphere that Joseph Kessel described during his search for slave markets with the smuggler Henry de Monfreid. At Port Sudan, I mused outside the abandoned yacht club, where virtually the

only vessels that berth there now are cargo boats. The Sudanese city is at once bustling and languid, enervated for several months of the year by the extreme heat and outrageous humidity. Gazing far out to sea, you spot *bateaux ivres,* "drunken boats," that could be the vessels that carried Rimbaud on his quest, searching like Lawrence of Arabia for the desert and its epic cavalcades. You picture Ibn Battuta, born in Tangier in the early fourteenth century, setting sail after journeying up the Nile Valley, on his way to Jeddah and Mecca and his famous and astonishing travels. He was aware that seven centuries earlier these shores had cast up the unstoppable conquerors of the Maghreb, the Barbary Coast and Andalusia. For travelers on the Red Sea, the past was already a haunting presence.

Prevented from continuing his journey by a border war in the Sudan, Ibn Battuta was forced to turn back. His only possibility for boarding a ship was at Aidhab, the port from which North African pilgrims sailed for Mecca after the occupation of Palestine by the Crusaders. Instead, he decided to continue his journey overland, via Aqaba. After reaching Mecca at last, circa 1326 (year 726 of the Hegira), he left again on a camel. The pilgrims and caravans with whom he traveled to the shores of the Red Sea, meanwhile, benefited from the generosity.

When he reached the Red Sea, Ibn Battuta set sail on a dhow from Jeddah, heading in an unexpected direction, bound for the coast of Africa and the port of Sawakin.

ON THE TRAIL OF ADVENTURE

The Red Sea had thus become an Ariadne's thread mapping out the paths of adventures. Further south, the Sawakin of Ibn Battuta's time was like something out of a fairy tale. Today a little town in ruins, it stands on a circular coral island and is built of a combination of madrepore, or stony coral, extracted from the bed of the Red Sea, and lime plaster in a symphony of infinite shades of buff and pale cream. With no light pollution, the nights are made for navigating by the stars. The houses, with their doors in Javan teak and delicate stone carvings, are decaying: Archways are crumbling, and damaged vaults threaten to collapse under their own weight at any moment. Venerable cannons and ancient bombards evoke the wars of earlier times. A handful of surviving façades recall the splendors and glories of the past and of all the pomp of the dignitaries and great merchants of the Red Sea. A narrow inlet opens into the sea, as though beckoning mariners to race across the waves. On the Red Sea, as elsewhere, people die while the stones live on, but sometimes even whole towns can perish. The buff-colored sails of the boats seem to merge with the ancient sands of the surrounding desert. And new treasures constantly emerge.

Recently, several marine experts, scientists and environmentalists working for the Red Sea Development Company were diving along the Saudi coast when they discovered an important coral colony estimated to be more than six hundred years old. Situated in the south of Al-Waqadi Island, near Umluj, the colony is ten meters high. The discovery was the first of its kind in the Red Sea, and vital at a time when much of the coral around the world has been damaged by pollution and bleaching due to climate change and human activity. In the Kingdom, where strategies and policies are being adopted

to limit any interference in the marine system, several initiatives have been developed to protect the unique biodiversity there, especially on the seacoast. These initiatives focus on wildlife, fish livestock and marine life and on the enhancement of key natural habitats that support biodiversity and enable carbon sequestration. The results are real, such as the expansion of the fields of mangroves. The only woody plants that connect land and sea, mangroves also have their own ecosystems, with a very high capacity to absorb and bury CO_2 from the atmosphere. Large-scale plantation projects have been implemented. In Yanbu alone, mangrove cover has increased about fifty-fold since 1975, thanks to a large-scale rehabilitation project. As for underwater species, dugongs, turtles and dolphins are especially protected by the marine and environmental authorities.

In summer, the seashore offers the famous cool breeze from the Red Sea. From Al Wajh to Jeddah, the fishing boats show their splashes of color with hulls in red, green and blue, from which the fishermen sell their fresh fish for a handful of Saudi Riyals. The wooden fishing boats are reminders that for centuries the ports here hosted African pilgrims on the Hajj to Mecca. On both sides of the Red Sea, one can find old ports with buildings that reflect a patchwork of cultures and a swirling vortex of architectural styles, recalling the various phases of history in the area.

In the shallow waters along the Saudi coast, we can find coral reefs varying in width. These large underwater structures are composed of the skeletons of colonial marine invertebrates. Coral life is abundant and diverse, and sometimes, at low tide, white and rose ridges rise above the breaking waves. Coral formations are continuously growing. The Red Sea hosts nearly two hundred species of coral in its waters.

Attracted by the wonderful and nutritiously rich flora, more than a thousand species of fish have chosen this habitat. They are divisible into two main groups: the pelagic fish and the reef fish. One colorful member of the latter is the butterfly fish (Chaetodontidae family). A non-negligible proportion of the fish, about 15 percent, are endemic, meaning that they live only in the Red Sea area. For divers at any one of the Saudi spots, from Yanbu to Umluj or Al Wajh, there is always a chance of encountering fish species that they will not see elsewhere in the world.

Some of the species are solitary, living far from the others. Pelagic fish, which are mainly carnivorous, prefer to swim out in the open waters. But most species live in colonies or large schools, and prefer to stay close to the coral formations, which provide the required nutriments for survival. The diving sites on the Saudi coast are generally full of soft and hard coral, and colonies of barracuda, red snappers and many other species of fish gather there. The abundance of Red Sea fauna creates a wonderful world, able to attract more and more divers seeking reef walls, or even walkers who like to discover reefs from the shore. Only two types of equipment are necessary: good shoes or a diving snorkel.

You could almost imagine that you see, flying over those ancient dwellings, the hoopoe that served as messenger between King Solomon and the Queen of Sheba. These birds are as important in the Muslim imagination as the simurgh in the twelfth-century Persian poem *Conference of the Birds.* In the Islamic tradition, Solomon, or Sulaiman, is a prophet or prophet-king with supernatural powers. All that is missing is a storyteller to narrate one of the tales from *The Thousand and One Nights*, or perhaps a distant descendant of Sinbad the Sailor skimming the ramparts of Mocha on his way back to Basra.

JEWELS AND OTHER TREASURES OF THE RED SEA

I have put up my heels many times and in many places on the eastern coast, languishing in the heat. Sometimes waves of sand would pour into the streets like breakers rolling in from the desert. That happens when the Red Sea shoreline is being swept by the khamsin, a hot, dry, dusty wind that's like the sirocco and turns the sky orange. Considered to be divine in origin, the wind blows large quantities of desert sand over land and sea. In the 1930s, the writer and correspondent Joseph Kessel, in a quest for the "burning shores of the Red Sea" (*Fortune Carrée*), discovered a previously unsuspected passion for adventure, guided by his friend Henry de Monfreid, a smuggler who would himself soon turn to writing. André Malraux hurried off to follow in Kessel's footsteps, searching for ruins associated with the Queen of Sheba. Decades later, along came another brilliant writer, Romain Gary. He had already spent many years as a diplomat, including at the United Nations in New York, and had won the Prix Goncourt, the most important French literary award. His experience would lead to *Les trésors de la mer Rouge*, a remarkable book that still inspires young writers today, another *Promise at Dawn*.

Writing for publications about the Red Sea, he displayed magnificent bursts of inspiration: "Already forty years ago I was constantly looking around in the hope of grasping the sudden and moving manifestation [of the human spirit], and it is these jewels, the only ones that nothing can ever deprive of their fabulous value and spellbinding power, that I bring back to you from the Red Sea and its region."

A born fabulist, gifted writer and nomad of multiple personalities, Gary completed the circuit of the Red Sea, taking his career from a novelist to the author of one of the earliest novels concerned with ecology, *The Roots of Heaven*, and then a diplomat. During his multiple lives he more than once covered his tracks in order to forge his own destiny and trace that of the world. With these writers on their travels, once again the world of the imagination comes into the service of reportage, and truth turns out to be stranger than fiction. My thoughts turn to the desert mirages on both shores of the Red Sea, on the coasts of Africa and of Arabia Felix, when the heat haze transforms the coastal desert into dreamlike waves. It was on the shores of the Red Sea that Gary found what he had been seeking for decades, "what remains of millennia, kingdoms and empires when they vanish down the centuries: the indefinable survival of a transient moment."

A SALTWATER OASIS, LUSH IN FLORA AND FAUNA

Rarely do the depths of the sea present an environment that is truly evocative of what we see on land—but it does happen off the Sinai Peninsula, and not by chance. The red coral found there has its echo in the high walls of the surrounding region. The flame-red sponges recall the mountains around the Monastery of St. Catherine, in their shades of pink, yellow and gray. Farther south, the stinging yellow and orange fire corals that flourish in the depths mirror the mountains of the Hejaz. The smooth walls of deep-sea gorges

mirror the mountains of the Hejaz. The smooth walls of deep-sea gorges plunge into canyons, scoured over the millennia. And the soft gorgonian corals are like miniature palm trees lost in a saltwater oasis, lush in its flora and fauna.

In the Red Sea, just offshore from the Saudi city of Jazan and its famous Corniche Park, lies another treasure: the Farasan Islands, a marine sanctuary on the Arabian continental shelf. The archipelago boasts more than 170 islands and islets, which are rich in flora and fauna. Feluccas and sambuks found shelter there in centuries past, before they were forgotten. Formed from uplifted fossil coral reefs, the islands are today part of a UNESCO World Heritage site, an incredible marine reserve with manta rays, hawksbill turtles, dolphins and other species living in the shallow coral reefs.

Just as the desert has its own poetry, familiar to the travelers and nomads of the Sahara, there is a poetry of the Red Sea. It has attracted travelers, adventurers and conquerors. Its crossings are often dramatic, but they are also epic, Homeric in nature. The Red Sea likes to remind us that it washes away the traces of its pioneers to demonstrate which is stronger: the sea, not humanity. It is true that in the north, on the heights of Mount Sinai, the region became the cradle of monotheistic religions when, according to the Old Testament, Moses, or Musa, received the tablets of the law as lightning bolts fell from the sky.

THE RED SEA TODAY

Attracting vacationers with its ideal swimming weather year-round, the Saudi coast of the Red Sea reveals both old and new jewels. Among the more recent: diving activities, including snorkeling, along preserved shores where the integrity of the fauna and flora is ensured, as well as around islands of rare coral that appear as ridges and barrier-like reefs. Along the Saudi coast, the longest on the Red Sea, we can find unique world-class diving sites, in particular in Sharm Obhur, where it is easy for beginners and the more advanced to enter the sea from the shore. Once you are in the water, lionfish, turtles, eels and clown fish will kindly greet you. For the most temerarious divers and fans of submarine adventure, it is possible to approach various kinds of sharks, even the rare bull shark, but only when accompanied by a local guide to guarantee safety. An extraordinary experience, too, is swimming with the rare hawksbill turtles, and alongside green sea turtles, among the largest on the planet, named for the greenish color of their cartilage.

Duba, to the north, deserves its local nickname, "the Pearl of the Red Sea." And from this quiet city, travelers and divers can discover the charming Al Numan island, with ancient archaeological sites, many of them hitherto unexplored.

The part of the Red Sea coast described so far is a perfect base camp for adventure travelers, offering undiscovered diving destinations and exciting trips inland among the sweeping desert dunes. The northern sections of the Saudi coastline not only have excellent diving and swimming sites but also shipwrecks, which attract additional fauna and flora to their unique environments, sometimes sheltering untouched marine life. As a new trend, hiking groups have been forming a short distance from the coast—as the spectacular views, particularly in the Hejaz region, thrill even the most seasoned climbers. The Bedouin camps are a must for those who love the wilderness and want to discover life in the desert, with its old traditions and the best—and most ecological—means of transportation in the region: the camel. To ride one is a fabulous experience, among the things to do at least once in a lifetime! Bedouins show their legendary hospitality, with tea, a bowl full of delicious dates from the next palm grove and traditional songs of welcome. Camels loaded with tents and supplies will transport travelers wherever and whenever they want to go, with Bedouin guides who know the way by heart. Dune bashing is an option, and later in the evening one gets to experience the tradition of storytelling: Bedouins orally passing down tales and folklore through the generations, another way in which the Kingdom can highlight its culture to the world.

Farther down the coast is Umluj, a remote locale for those who prefer solitude and a quiet stay but with all the adventures of both desert and sea. Its rich culture is crystallized in the goat-hair tents and patterned rugs. Just offshore lie small islands that seem to be still unknown. And here one can find the adventurous spirit of the Red Sea, reminiscent of *The Arabian Nights* as told in folklore. Swimmers and divers can easily head by small boat to these sandy and coral-fringed islands. Sometimes, one can encounter a coral colony, home to a huge number of fish and other marine life—a kind of magical submarine forest.

In the middle of this coastline is the King Abdullah Economic City (KAEC), wedged between the sands of the desert and the sands of the seashore. This astonishing city, a kind of "smart city" of the twenty-first century, is divided into small residential, commercial and recreational areas, and represents a

vivid example of a modern and holistic urbanization, with its equestrian club, yacht club and golf course. And new jobs are being created there every week. It combines good access and accommodations with the possibilities of desert trips and wildlife experiences in the backcountry.

Continuing south, one reaches Jeddah. Throughout its history Jeddah was the first stop for many pilgrims on their way to Mecca. Today it is a veritable hub of heritage and modernity, perfectly blended. Jeddah offers another surprise, a port open to the world for centuries and some of the best coastal experiences in the Kingdom. Emerging from the coastline, the floating Al Rahma Mosque is literally built on the water. Although Jeddah is mainly a modern town, it does preserve its past, and UNESCO has included the historic center, which dates to the seventh century, on its list of World Heritage sites. More recently, Jeddah has evolved into the art capital of Saudi Arabia.

For those who prefer to discover these beautiful sites from the open sea, several cruises are available, from north to south, from Al Wajh to Umluj and Jeddah—with nearly two dozen itineraries. With its swimming and diving areas, archaeological sites, waters full of marine life, and wonderful vistas, the Kingdom is an ideal travel destination.

AS I EXPLORED THE RED SEA, I EXPERIENCED A METAMORPHOSIS

This interweaving of the human and the divine has survived the depredations of time, though at the cost of a certain amount of exegesis. Transforming hopes into holy writ is a distinguishing characteristic of the melting pot that is the Red Sea. Viewed from the summit of one of its coastal mountains, its two shores—Africa on one side and Arabia on the other—appear to be reaching out to each other, the Christian festivities and underground churches of Ethiopia and the minarets and architectural wonders of the Arab coast, the camel riders of the desert and the mariners in their dhows. The most ancient kings in the world, who lived here and sent their dhows across the waters, knew their names would live on in history.

Twenty centuries after the reign of the Queen of Sheba, the mystery of the Red Sea continues to exert its power. And the emotions of the voyage, from the first sightings of Suez to the Bab-el-Mandeb Strait ("Gate of Tears"), and from the Straits of Tiran to the Farasan Islands, remain unchanged, just as in Rimbaud's time. I was fortunate enough to meet another poet who had traveled to the region, though long after Rimbaud. That was Philippe Soupault, and our encounter took place shortly before his death in 1990. One of the founders of the surrealist movement, along with Louis Aragon and André Breton, Soupault chose to escape the salons of Paris to explore the Muslim world in the 1950s. "The Red Sea is a magnet that has attracted and held on to men who would overthrow the foundations of the world," he wrote in 1982. One of the first to travel in Rimbaud's footsteps, Soupault visited ports of call in the holy land of Islam. Later, he described this odyssey as a genuine rebirth, a transformation of self: "The person I thought I was

no longer resembled me." And in an impressive and eloquent declaration for a poet at odds with the status quo, he said, "As I explored the Red Sea, I experienced a metamorphosis." That is the ultimate dream of the writer-traveler, and one that still inspires so many.

May the dream live on through the generations, in this alchemy of the elsewhere and the shared living space. May this sea, fringed by the perfumes of Arabia and the fragrance of incense, become once more a bridge connecting cultures, religions and civilizations.

Among these jewels, one can find unknown sites and adventurous spots, still very protected in terms of the environment. In the northwest, Saudi Arabia likes to reveal its past and its modern aspects, attracting travelers who want to enjoy both desert trips and diving. Off the coast, at Al Wajh, we can find an archipelago of pristine islands. In the backcountry, cultural treasures challenge mountain peaks and ancient dormant volcanoes that mark important merchant trading routes dating back thousands of years. And Al Wajh is the perfect gateway to AlUla, which contains the Kingdom's archaeological centerpiece: Hegra, a UNESCO World Heritage site, with a complex of tombs laid out by the Nabataeans in the first century BCE and the first century CE.

In Yanbu, surrounded by intensely turquoise waters, the almost untouched coral reefs and the sand seem to marry. Fishermen slowly approach with their boats, walking on the one-meter-deep coral plateau, the seabed appearing so close to the surface that they might catch fish with their bare hands. In Saudi

Arabia, coral reefs and their surrounding environments are heavily protected, under a policy to develop ecological diversity in the area. Endowed with such an impressive and, more importantly, thriving biodiversity, including many unique species, Saudi Arabia has prioritized the creation of several preservation initiatives, some of which have already been undertaken. Among them is the Marine Science program launched by King Abdullah University of Science and Technology, north of Jeddah. Creating a living laboratory with great potential, this project is developing an integrated understanding of the Red Sea's ecosystem and coral farming, with research achievements in biology, particularly on the symbiosis of algae and prokaryotes. As for the Red Sea Development Company, the approach of the program is holistic, encompassing research, tourism and the local economy, based on sustainable development.

The Saudi Diving Center, in Yanbu, invites visitors to enjoy the best spots in that area, among gorgonian coral reefs. Off the coast, an easy day trip away, there is a series of coral reefs called "the Seven Sisters," which are famous for their structures and wonderful colors. Inland, a forty-minute drive from the coast, fans of archaeology can discover the incredible city of Yanbu Al Nakhal, founded more than two thousand years ago.

The Red Sea is truly "an ocean in the making," marked by the separation between the African and Arabian tectonic plates, which are still moving, the shores distancing themselves at the rate of about two centimeters each year. But it is also a magical place, a mirror held up to the Mediterranean. And so much of it remains to be explored, or even imagined.

" The first thing you notice when you visit the island is, of course, the pristine environment, with clear turquoise waters, white sand and an abundance of coral reefs. "

Kengo Kuma, *architect*

" When I swam through, I found myself in a magical underwater palace. **"**

Ethan Todras-Whitehill, *journalist*

"The Red Sea is thus a melting pot of civilizations, faiths and hopes."

Christopher Smith, *writer*

" The Red Sea is a magnet that has attracted and held on to men who would overthrow the foundations of the world. "

Philippe Soupault, *writer*

" A thousand Dreams within me softly burn. "

Arthur Rimbaud, *poet*

" From birth, man carries the weight of gravity on his shoulders. He is bolted to earth. But man has only to sink beneath the surface and he is free. "

Jacques Cousteau, *marine explorer*

6 6 From the very
first encounter,
I was entranced
by its crystalline
clarity, its dizzying
transparency
(reaching down
two hundred meters
in places) and its
pristine coral reefs. **9 9**

Christopher Smith, *writer*

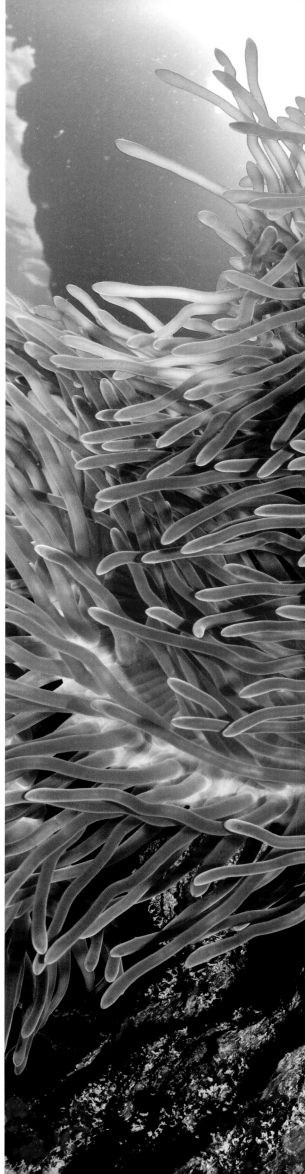

66 Each dive is different, but the same silence sings. 99

Chris Leidy, *photographer*

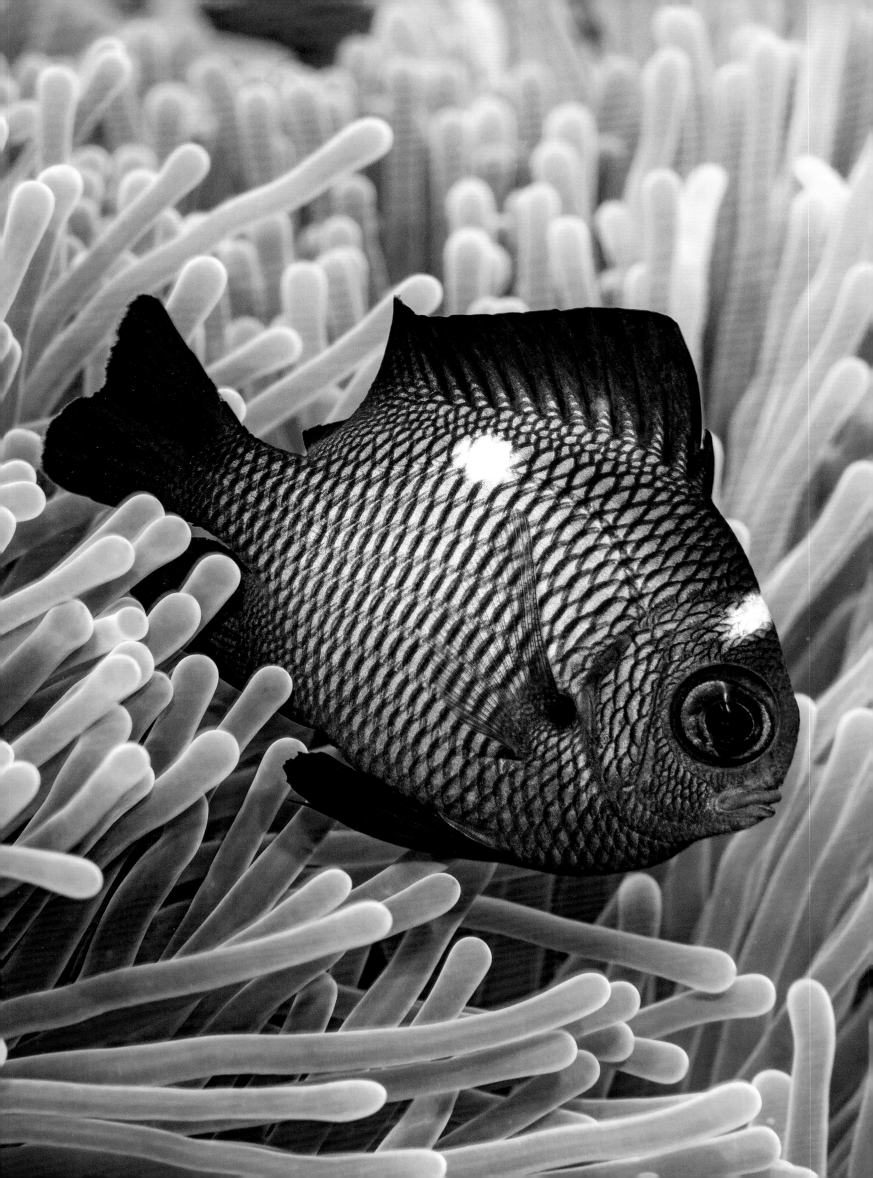

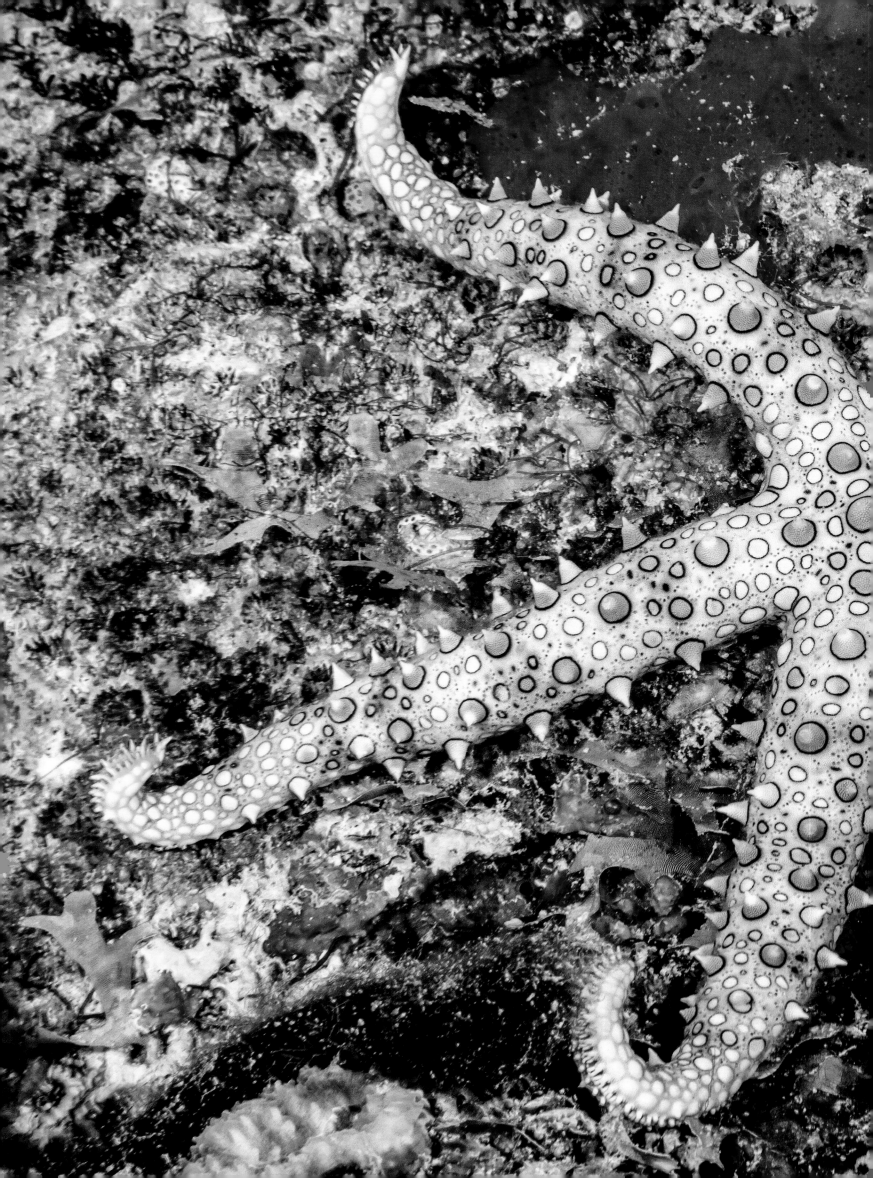

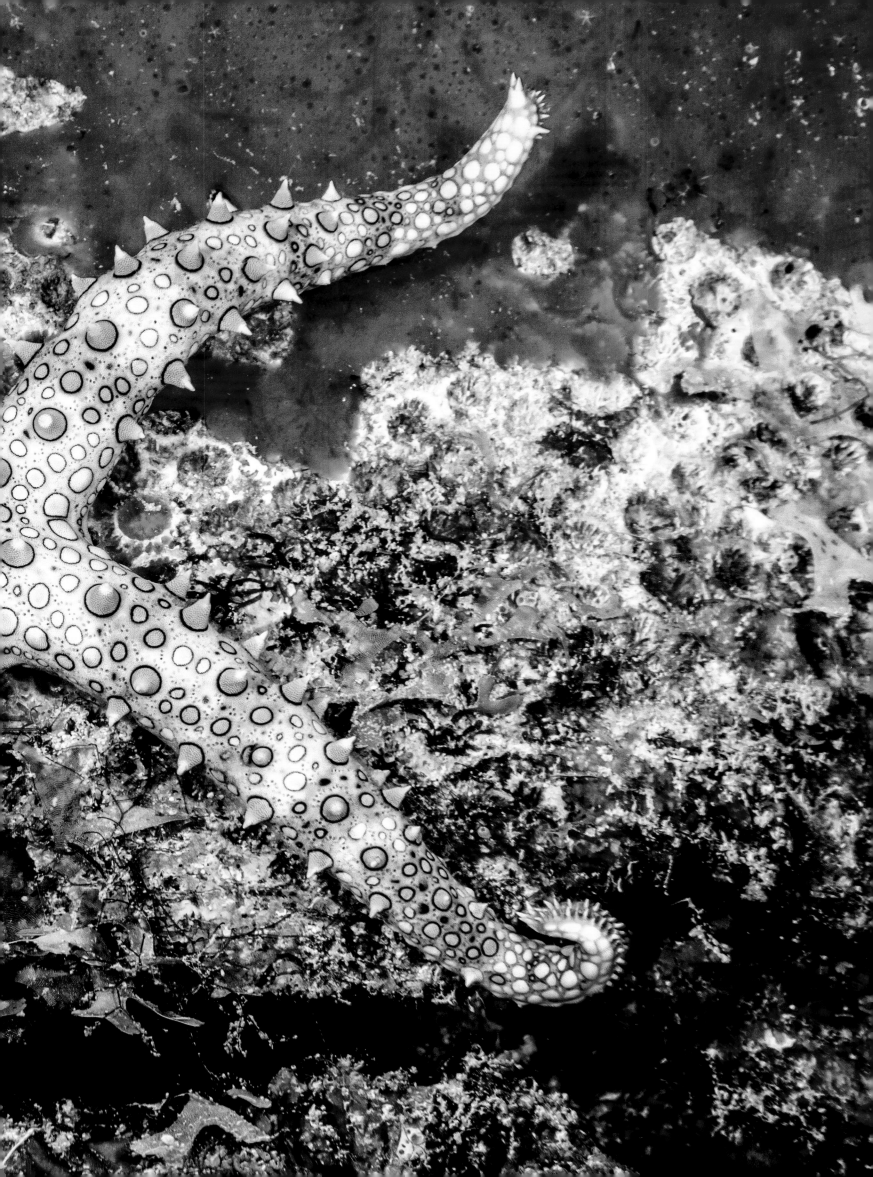

" There's something about laidback beach towns boasting bohemian vibes that enchant my soul. Dahab does not disappoint in serving up an abundance of unique cafes with impeccable views of the Red Sea. "

Iliah Grant-Altoro, *writer*